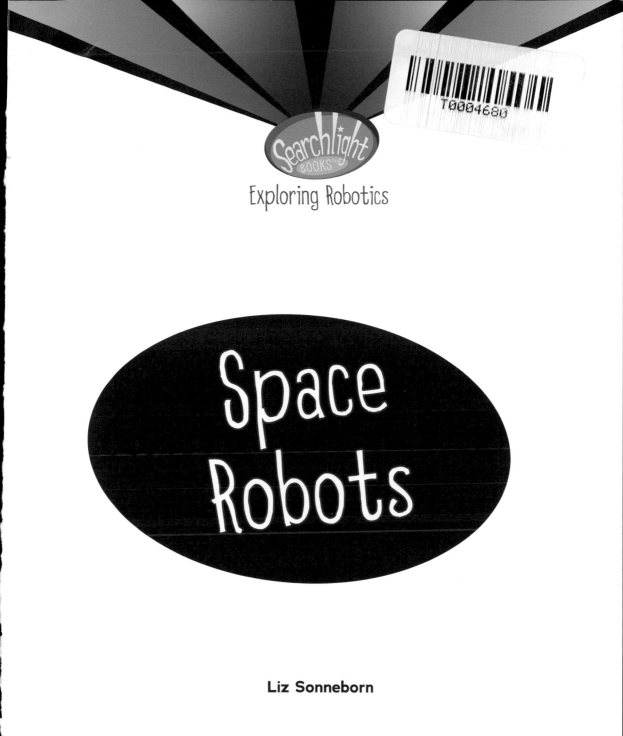

Searchlight
BOOKS™

Exploring Robotics

Space Robots

Liz Sonneborn

Lerner Publications ◆ Minneapolis

To Robyn

Lerner Publications Company
An imprint of Lerner Publishing Group, Inc.
241 First Avenue North
Minneapolis, MN 55401 USA

For reading levels and more information, look up this title at www.lernerbooks.com.

Main body text set in Adrianna Regular.
Typeface provided by Chank.

Editor: Lauren Foley

Library of Congress Cataloging-in-Publication Data

Names: Sonneborn, Liz, author.
Title: Space robots / Liz Sonneborn.
Description: Minneapolis : Lerner Publications, [2024] | Series: Searchlight books. Exploring robotics | Includes bibliographical references and index. | Audience: Ages 8–11 | Audience: Grades 4–6 | Summary: "Robots can take photos, navigate tough terrain, and carry cargo—all while in outer space! From their role in the 1950s space race to helping map Mars, find out more about space robots"— Provided by publisher.
Identifiers: LCCN 2022038299 (print) | LCCN 2022038300 (ebook) | ISBN 9781728476810 (library binding) | ISBN 9798765600238 (ebook)
Subjects: LCSH: Space robotics—Juvenile literature. | Robots—Juvenile literature.
Classification: LCC TL1097 .S625 2024 (print) | LCC TL1097 (ebook) | DDC 629.8/92—dc23/eng/20221004

LC record available at https://lccn.loc.gov/2022038299
LC ebook record available at https://lccn.loc.gov/2022038300

Manufactured in the United States of America
1-52287-50702-10/31/2022

Table of Contents

Chapter 1

EXPLORERS AND HELPERS

For more than sixty years, astronauts have traveled to space. They have orbited Earth and landed on the moon. They have performed many experiments. Astronauts help scientists understand the universe.

But much of what we know about space comes from a different source—robots! Robots are machines that perform certain tasks. Some can work on their own. Others need instructions from people to do their jobs.

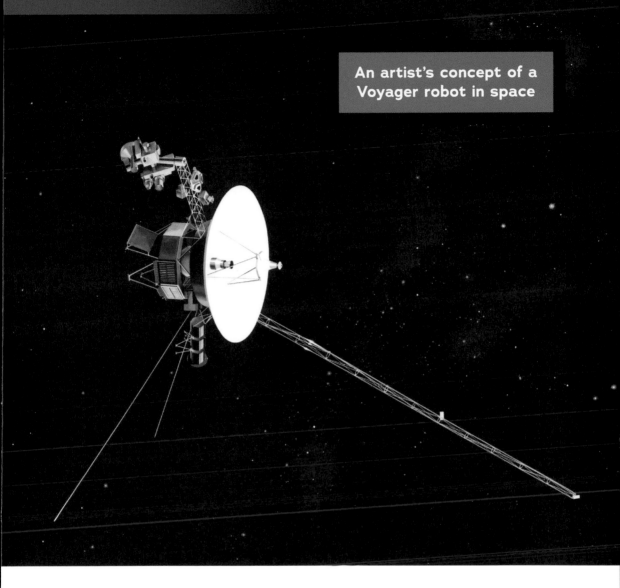

An artist's concept of a Voyager robot in space

Hardy Workers

Space robots come in all shapes and sizes. They may be as large as a car or as small as a shoebox. They often have computers and sensors that collect information about their surroundings. They might also have antennae. Antennae allow them to send radio signals to Earth.

All space robots are hard workers. Many travel vast distances. Some orbit moons and planets to gather data about them. Others land on moons and planets to collect soil samples and take photographs. Robots also help astronauts on space missions. They repair and build equipment and help perform experiments.

Robots help repair spacecraft.

Space robots are tough. They need to be sturdy enough to operate under harsh conditions such as extreme temperatures and low gravity. Rovers that travel on planets and moons handle rough terrain. They must be able to navigate cliffs, canyons, and icy surfaces.

Upper Mount Shar

Gale Crater – Northern Rim

Vera Rubin Ridge

Gale Crater floor

Glen Etive 2

Glen Etive 1

Rovers and other space robots have to handle harsh conditions such as rough terrain.

Space Robots vs. Astronauts

Scientists use space robots for many reasons. For example, humans cannot survive in all space

environments. On some planets, extreme temperatures and high radiation levels could hurt or kill astronauts. But well-built robots have no trouble operating there.

Astronauts must eat, sleep, and go to the bathroom. But robots do not have these needs. This makes planning their trips much simpler.

Astronauts need special suits to stay safe in space.

A ROBOTIC ARM HELPING MOVE EQUIPMENT ABOARD THE INTERNATIONAL SPACE STATION

Scientists also do not have to bring robots back home. After robots break down, many just stay in space.

Astronauts have helped us learn a lot about space. But using robots to explore space is cheaper, easier, and safer.

Chapter 2

THE RACE FOR SPACE

On October 4, 1957, the Soviet Union sent Sputnik 1 into space. This satellite became the first human-made object to orbit Earth. The race to control space had begun.

The US government was afraid it was losing the space race. It turned to the National Aeronautics and Space Administration (NASA). The government tasked NASA with sending the first astronauts to the moon.

To the Moon and Mars

NASA built robots to make the moon landing possible. Beginning in 1966, it sent Surveyor spacecraft to the moon's surface. They landed safely, proving the surface was solid. They also took thousands of photographs.

A photo of Surveyor 1's shadow on the moon's surface taken by the robot

This information helped NASA plan a mission for astronauts. On July 20, 1969, two American astronauts became the first humans on the moon. Thanks to the Surveyor robots, they knew what to expect and how to land safely.

Buzz Aldrin, one of the first humans on the moon, walks on its surface.

VIKING 1 BEING LAUNCHED ON THE CENTAUR ROCKET IN 1975

NASA began using robots to explore other planets. In 1975, Viking 1 and 2 flew to Mars. Each craft had a lander and an orbiter. The landers looked for signs of life on the planet's surface. The orbiters took pictures of Mars from space.

Spirit and Opportunity were Mars rovers. They taught scientists a lot about Mars.

In 1997, NASA launched the Sojourner rover to Mars. This small, wheeled robot could travel on the surface. It paved the way for larger Mars rovers such as Spirit and Opportunity in 2003. In 2011, Opportunity made an amazing discovery. The rover found a rock that contained the elements zinc and bromine. The elements suggested that water had once flowed on Mars.

Key Figure

When Donna Shirley was in college, her adviser told her girls could not be engineers. Engineers build machines and technology. Shirley's thirty-two-year career at NASA's Jet Propulsion Laboratory proved him wrong. With Jacob Matijevic, she led the team that built Sojourner. In 1997, it became the first robot on Mars. It was supposed to work for seven days. But it kept operating for eighty-three. Its design became a model for bigger, more advanced Mars rovers.

To Faraway Planets and Beyond

Voyager 1 and 2 have traveled even farther. Launched in 1977, these robots have flown by Jupiter, Saturn, Uranus, and Neptune. They have sent back close-up, color photographs of these planets and their moons.

In 2012, Voyager 1 became the first human-made craft to enter interstellar space—the space between stars. Voyager 2 followed in 2018. These robots are billions of miles from Earth and will continue their missions until about 2025.

An artist's depiction of Voyager 1 entering interstellar space

Chapter 3

SPACE ROBOTS TODAY

Every day, scientists design, build, and program new space robots to take on fresh challenges. One of the most impressive new robots is Perseverance. This rover touched down on Mars on February 18, 2021. Perseverance's mission is to search for signs of past life. The rover has a drill to take soil samples. Then it seals them in tubes. The samples will someday return to Earth to be analyzed.

A-PUFFER WAS DESIGNED TO FIT IN TIGHT AREAS.

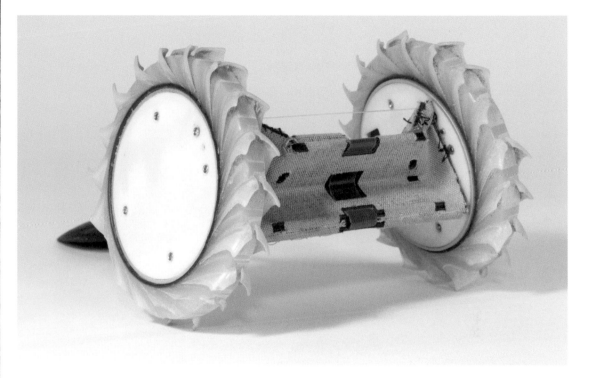

New Designs

A-PUFFER is another robot explorer. This tiny, wheeled vehicle can go to hard-to-reach craters and cramped caves on the moon. Its wheels can bend down to make it almost flat. This helps it move through the tightest spaces.

LEMUR was the first in a family of robots designed to climb and crawl. It has four limbs and sixty-four fingers. Each finger is covered with hundreds of hooks. These hooks allow LEMUR to grab onto and climb rock walls.

LEMUR inspired two newer robots. Ice Worm looks like one LEMUR limb. On icy surfaces, it can move like an inchworm. RoboSimian is shaped like LEMUR, but it has four wheels. It can crawl over rough terrain, slide on its underside, and even spin cartwheels.

LEMUR climbing a wall

Robots such as Canadarm2 help move equipment and astronauts around the ISS.

On the ISS

The International Space Station (ISS) orbits Earth. The astronauts who live and work there rely on robot helpers. One is Canadarm2, an almost 58-foot (18 m) robotic arm. It helps move supplies, grabs orbiting spacecraft for repair missions, and more. At each end of Canadarm2 are handlike tools that can grip objects. They sometimes guide astronauts on space walks.

Robonaut 2 spent seven years aboard the ISS. This robot looks like the upper body of a person. It has a head, torso, and arms. Robonaut 2's humanlike hands allowed it to repair equipment on the ISS.

ISS astronauts are also assisted by three Astrobees. These cube-shaped robots help with routine chores such as photographing experiments and moving cargo. The Astrobees are named Honey, Queen, and Bumble. These busy robots buzz through the air like bees as they work.

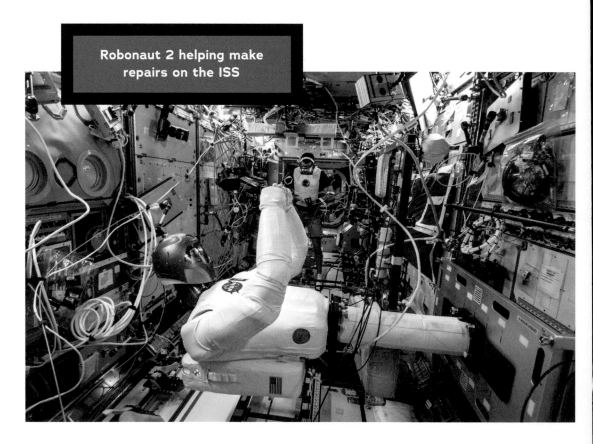

Robonaut 2 helping make repairs on the ISS

STEM Spotlight

Scientists communicate with space robots through the Deep Space Network. It has giant antennae all around the world. Antennae operators precisely point them toward the robots. Then they send commands through radio waves. Space robots also use radio waves to send photographs and data back to Earth. Radio waves travel very fast—186,000 miles (299,338 km) per second! But it can still take more than twenty hours for a message to reach a faraway spacecraft.

Chapter 4

INTO THE FUTURE

In upcoming years, space will be a busy place. Many
countries, such as the US, China, and Russia, are planning
space missions. Private companies such as SpaceX are
working to launch spacecraft too. All their plans involve
space robots.

The Lunar Gateway

The Lunar Gateway is planned to launch no earlier than late 2024. This small space station would orbit the moon. It would be a stopping point for astronauts on lunar missions. Astronauts would stay there for a few weeks each year. Robots would keep the station running the rest of the time.

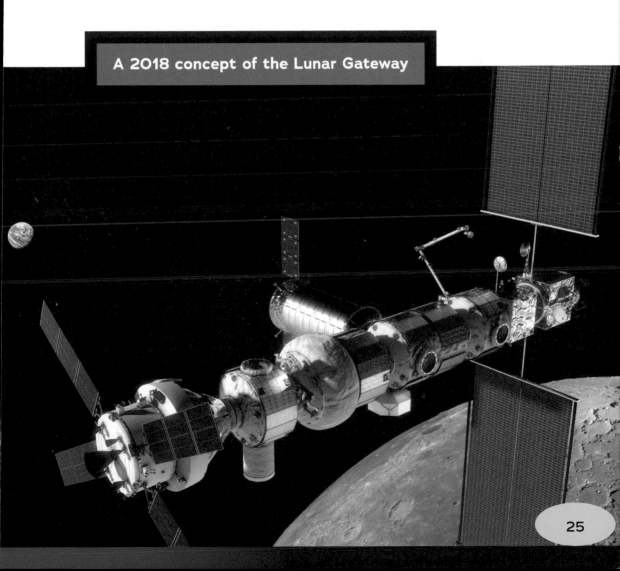

A 2018 concept of the Lunar Gateway

Perseverance took many photos on Mars such as this one inside a crater.

Someday the Lunar Gateway may be a stopover for astronauts heading to Mars. Scientists are planning a mission to send people to the planet. Space robots are already hard at work to make it possible. The Mars rover Perseverance photographs the planet's surface, measures the terrain, and looks for dangerous areas. This information will help scientists plan for humans to land on Mars.

Tomorrow's Space Robots

People will probably not be able to go to more far-off moons and planets anytime soon. But robots will. For example, NASA plans to launch Dragonfly in 2026. This robot spacecraft will travel eight years before reaching Titan, Saturn's largest moon. It will search for signs of life there.

Scientists are developing robots to maintain and build equipment in space. NASA's OSAM-1 mission will use a robotic arm to refuel a satellite. SPIDER will be aboard too. This robot will construct a seven-piece antenna in space. Similar robots may one day be able to build entire space stations.

An artist's depiction of Dragonfly on Titan

STEM Spotlight

Asteroids and comets are hard to explore with a wheeled rover because they have very low gravity. A rover's wheels have trouble getting traction on them. As a rover rolls, it can easily flip upside down. Scientists have solved this problem with a new type of rover. Hedgehog is a small, cube-shaped robot. It moves by hopping and tumbling. Hedgehog can also spin into the air. This move keeps the robot from getting stuck in sandpits.

Robots such as the arm
on the ISS will continue
to help astronauts.

Newer space robots are getting smarter.
Many are designed with artificial intelligence.
This allows them to learn and make decisions.
They might soon be better at solving complex
problems than astronauts are.

It's hard to predict what future space
explorations will find. But space robots will play
a big role in many new discoveries.

Glossary

antenna: a metal rod that can send and receive radio signals

interstellar: between stars

lander: a spacecraft designed to land on the surface of a body in space such as a planet or moon

orbit: to move in a circle around another object

orbiter: a spacecraft designed to orbit a body such as a planet in space without landing on its surface

radiation: waves or particles of energy

rover: a vehicle that can move on the surface of a planet or moon

satellite: a human-made object that orbits Earth or another body in space

Soviet Union: a former country made up of fifteen republics including Russia

space station: a large satellite where astronauts can perform experiments

Learn More

Britannica Kids: Mars Exploration Rover
   https://kids.britannica.com/kids/article/Mars-Exploration-Rover
   /544857

Parks, Spencer. *Robots in Space.* New York: Cavendish Square, 2022.

Smibert, Angie. *Space Robots.* Minneapolis: Core Library, 2019.

Thomas, Rachael L. *Revolutionary Robots in Space.* Minneapolis: Lerner
   Publications, 2020.

What Is Robotics?
   https://www.nasa.gov/audience/forstudents/k-4/stories/nasa-knows
   /what_is_robotics_k4.html

Why Do We Send Robots to Space?
   https://spaceplace.nasa.gov/space-robots/en/

Index

Photo Acknowledgments

Image credits: NASA/JPL, p. 5; NASA Goddard/Chris Gunn, p. 6; NASA/JPL-Caltech/MSSS,
p. 7; Motokoka/Wikipedia, p. 8; NASA, pp. 9, 11, 12, 13, 14, 20, 21, 22, 25, 29; Bob Riha Jr./Getty
Images, p. 15; NASA/JPL-Caltech, pp. 16, 17, 19; NASA/JPL-Caltech/ASU/MSSS, p. 26; NASA/
Johns Hopkins APL, p. 27.

Cover: Boyer/Roger Viollet/Getty Images.